FANTASTIC FACTS ABOUT

DINOSAURS

Author
Jinny Johnson

Editor
Elizabeth Gogerly

Design
Tessa Barwick

Index
Caroline Hamilton

Editorial Co-ordination
Lynda Lines

Editorial Assistance
Jenny Siklós

This is a Parragon Book
First published in 2000

Parragon, Queen Street House, 4 Queen Street, Bath BA1 1HE, UK

Copyright © Parragon 2000

Produced by Monkey Puzzle Media Ltd
Gissing's Farm, Fressingfield, Suffolk IP21 5SH, UK

All rights reserved. No part of this publication may be reproduced, stored in a retrieval system, or transmitted by any means, electronic, mechanical, photocopying, recording or otherwise, without the prior permission of the copyright holder.

ISBN 0-75253-166-2

Printed in Italy

FANTASTIC FACTS ABOUT

DINOSAURS

p

CONTENTS

WHAT ARE DINOSAURS? 6
The Dinosaur World 8
How Do We Know About Dinosaurs? 10
The Dinosaur Hunters 12

DINOSAUR LIFE STYLES 14
Dinosaur Families 16

MEAT-EATING DINOSAURS 18
Tetanurans 20
Maniraptorans 22
Ornithomimids 24
Tyrannosaurs 26

Plant-Eating Dinosaurs 28
Sauropods 30
Boneheaded Dinosaurs 32
Fabrosaurs and Hypsilophodonts 34
Iguanodonts 36
Duckbilled Dinosaurs 38
What are Stegosaurs? 40
Armoured Dinosaurs 42
Parrot Dinosaurs and Early Horned Dinosaurs 44
Later Horned Dinosaurs 46

Other Reptiles 48
Plesiosaurs and Pliosaurs 50
Ichthyosaurs 52
Pterosaurs 54
Pterodactyls 56
Mammal-Like Reptiles 58

The End Of The Dinosaurs 60

Index 62

INTRODUCTION TO

WHAT ARE DINOSAURS?

Dinosaurs are the most extraordinary and successful animals that have ever lived. They first evolved about 230 million years ago and dominated life on Earth until they died out about 65 million years ago.

Dinosaurs were reptiles. The name dinosaur means "terrible lizard" from the Greek *deinos*, meaning "terrible" and sauros meaning "lizard". They were given this name because the first discoverers of dinosaur bones realized that they came from a type of reptile and thought they must have belonged to giant lizards. Gradually, as more fossil bones were found, experts realized that these were not just huge lizards but a different type of reptile altogether.

Like most reptiles today, dinosaurs had bony skeletons, leathery skin and reproduced by laying eggs. Some killed other creatures to eat; others fed on plants. All dinosaurs lived on land – creatures such as flying pterosaurs and swimming ichthyosaurs that lived at the same time were reptiles but not dinosaurs.

ORNITHISCHIAN DINOSAURS
The two types of dinosaurs differed in the structure of their hip-bones. In ornithischian dinosaurs the pubis bone was below and running parallel with the hip-joint. All ornithischian dinosaurs were plant eaters. They included dinosaurs such as stegosaurs, ankylosaurs and iguanodonts.

Both hip-bones pointing downward and backwards.

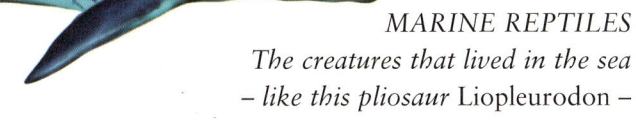

MARINE REPTILES
The creatures that lived in the sea – like this pliosaur Liopleurodon *– were not dinosaurs.*

One reason that dinosaurs survived longer than earlier reptiles was that they moved more efficiently. Early reptiles moved with their legs sprawled out to the sides and their belly close to the ground, like crocodiles and lizards today. The legs of dinosaurs were positioned more or less straight down under the body, like those of mammals. This meant the dinosaurs could carry more weight, take bigger steps and move faster.

SAURISCHIAN DINOSAURS
In saurischian dinosaurs the pubis bone pointed away from the hip-joint. The saurischians split into two groups – plant eaters and meat eaters. The plant eaters included the giant sauropods such as Diplodocus, *while the meat eaters included fierce hunters such as* Tyrannosaurus.

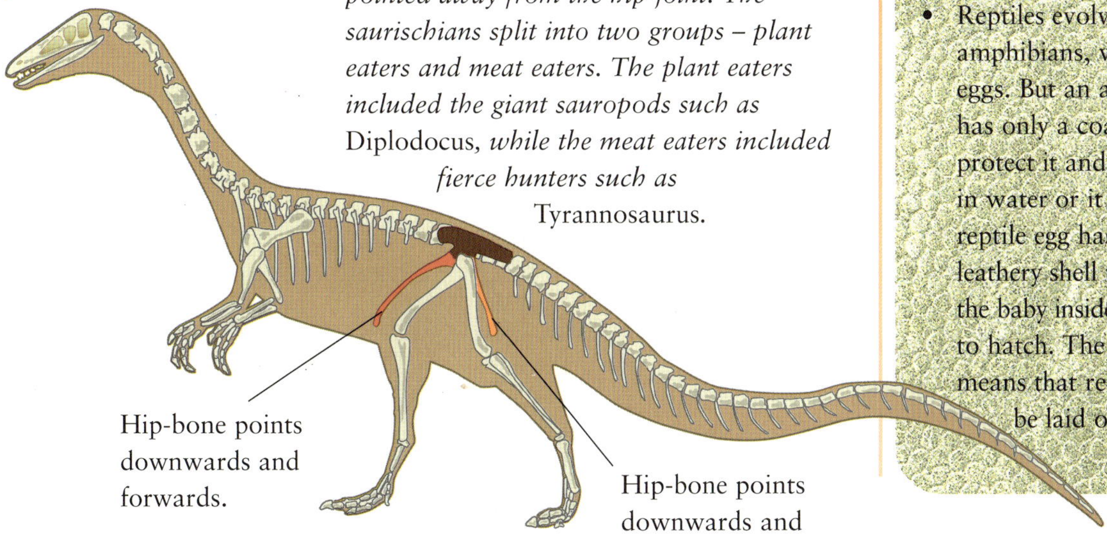

Hip-bone points downwards and forwards.

Hip-bone points downwards and backwards.

Sizing up the dinosaurs
- At present, about 500 different species of dinosaurs are known. These can be divided into two groups known as saurischians and ornithischians which have different kinds of skeletons.
- Dinosaurs ranged in size from creatures the size of a chicken to the giant sauropods which measured more than 30 metres (98 feet) long. A dinosaur found recently called *Argentinasaurus* may have measured as much as 49 metres (160 feet) long and 21 metres (69 feet) tall.

A good egg
- Reptiles evolved from amphibians, which also lay eggs. But an amphibian egg has only a coating of jelly to protect it and has to be laid in water or it dries out. A reptile egg has a hard or leathery shell that protects the baby inside until it is ready to hatch. The tough shell means that reptile eggs can be laid on land.

WHAT ARE DINOSAURS?

THE DINOSAUR WORLD

Dinosaurs first lived during the period known as the Triassic, which began 250 million years ago. The earliest dinosaurs were thought to be creatures such as *Eoraptor* and *Herrerasaurus* which lived in Argentina about 228 million years ago. In 1999, however, dinosaur remains were found in Madagascar which are thought to be even older, perhaps dating from about 230 million years ago.

TRIASSIC PERIOD
During the Triassic period all the world's land was joined together in one supercontinent, now called Pangaea, which means "all earth". This made it easy for the first dinosaurs to spread to all areas. The climate was warm and there were no ice caps. There were no flowering plants at this time and the land was covered with conifer trees and plants such as cycads, ferns and horse-tails.

JURASSIC PERIOD
By the Jurassic period, which began 208 million years ago, the world's land had started to break into two separate masses – now called Laurasia in the north and Gondwana in the south. The climate was wetter and slightly cooler but still warm, and conifers, ferns and cycads continued to thrive. Reptiles, particularly dinosaurs, were the dominant form of animal life. Smaller meat-eating dinosaurs hunted creatures such as lizards, insects and early mammals.

CRETACEOUS PERIOD
In the Cretaceous period, which began 146 million years ago, the landmasses continued to break up and the continents of today started to take shape. Sea levels rose and the oceans covered as much as a third of today's land area. Greater differences between the seasons were emerging and flowering plants began to take over from conifers, ferns and horse-tails. The greater variety of plants meant that there was more food for plant-eating dinosaurs and so many new kinds of dinosaur were able to evolve.

Other reptiles
- Alongside the first dinosaurs lived other kinds of reptiles, such as turtles and lizards, amphibians and fish.
- The first pterosaurs flew in the skies and marine reptiles, such as plesiosaurs and ichthyosaurs, inhabited the oceans.
- There were also many kinds of insects – many of which were relatives of common insects of today, such as the weta cricket.
- The dominant reptiles had been the group known as mammal-like reptiles. These began to decline, but one type of mammal-like reptile gave rise to mammals. The first mammals lived in the Late Triassic but by the beginning of the Jurassic, small, warm-blooded and hairy mammals, such as *Megazostrodon*, had begun to appear. There were not many mammals until the Cretaceous period.

How Do We Know About Dinosaurs?

No human has ever seen a living dinosaur, yet we know a surprizing amount about them. The main source of information has been the many fossils which have been found of dinosaur bones and teeth – fossils are the remains of dead animals preserved in rock. Dinosaur fossils have been discovered on every continent – even in Antarctica. Dinosaur experts, called palaeontologists, put these fossilized bones together to rebuild the skeletons of these long-dead creatures.

DINOSAUR FINDS
This map shows the major dinosaur finds across the modern world.

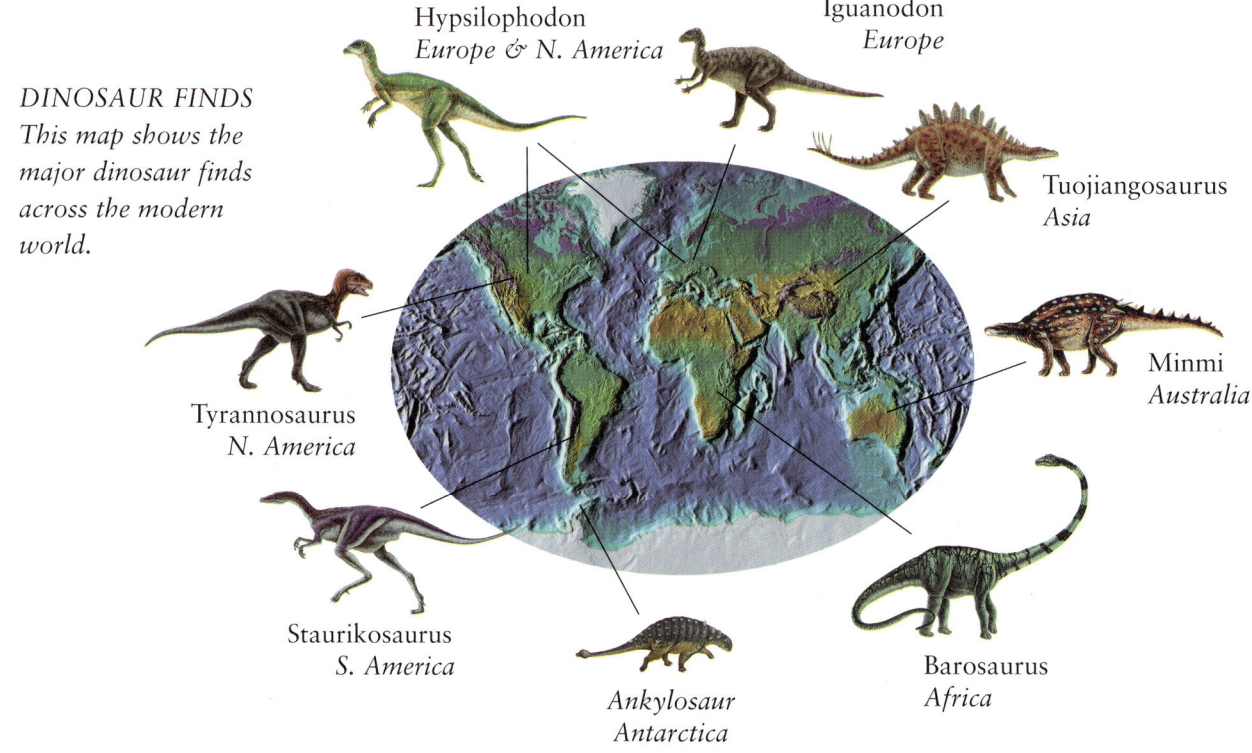

Hypsilophodon
Europe & N. America

Iguanodon
Europe

Tuojiangosaurus
Asia

Minmi
Australia

Tyrannosaurus
N. America

Staurikosaurus
S. America

Ankylosaur
Antarctica

Barosaurus
Africa

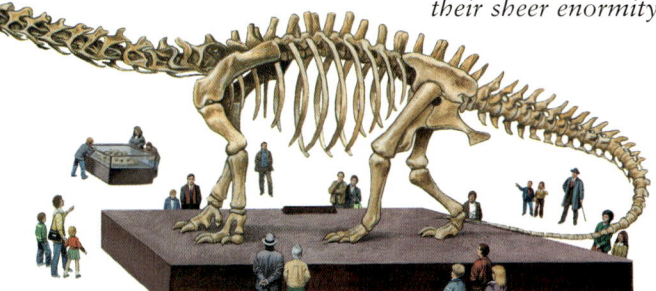

MUSEUM PIECE
Many dinosaur skeletons, such as this Diplodocus, *have been assembled in museums across the world for the public to see their sheer enormity.*

REBUILDING DINOSAURS

Usually only some of the bones of a dinosaur are discovered but the palaeontologists can use their knowledge of other similar dinosaurs and of the structure of creatures living today to recreate the missing parts. Marks on the bones show where muscles were attached in life and these marks help the experts flesh out the animal.

FOSSILIZATION
As dinosaurs died, their bones were often covered over by mud and other debris. The layers built up and hardened over the bones over thousands of years. Then millions of years later, erosion revealed the bones once again.

Fossils

- Fossils can also help experts to work out the animal's life style as well as its appearance. Fossilized teeth give experts clues about the sort of food a dinosaur might have eaten. Sharp or serrated teeth, for example, show that the animal was probably a meat-eating hunter. Long, slender leg bones usually mean the dinosaur was a fast runner.

But bones are not the only fossils. Fossilized footprints allow palaeontologists to work out how quickly a dinosaur might have moved and whether it travelled in herds. Some fossilized eggs and nests have been discovered that show us something about dinosaur breeding habits. Even fossilized dinosaur skin or dinosaur stomach contents have been discovered which help us to discover what the dinosaurs ate.

WHAT ARE DINOSAURS?

THE DINOSAUR HUNTERS

People have been finding dinosaur bones for thousands of years. There is even evidence that the ancient Chinese used dinosaur remains in their medicine. Dragons mentioned in ancient Chinese works were possibly reference to dinosaurs.

BONE FINDS
In 1824 an English geologist William Buckland found some jaw bones which he believed belonged to a reptile. He named the creature *Megalosaurus*, meaning "great lizard". At around the same time an English doctor, Gideon Mantell, and his wife discovered some large animal teeth.

FAMOUS DINOSAUR COLLECTORS
1 Othniel Marsh; 2 Dr Gideon Mantell; 3 Edward Drinker Cope; 4 Mary Mantell; 5 Dr Robert Plot; 6 Sir Richard Owen.

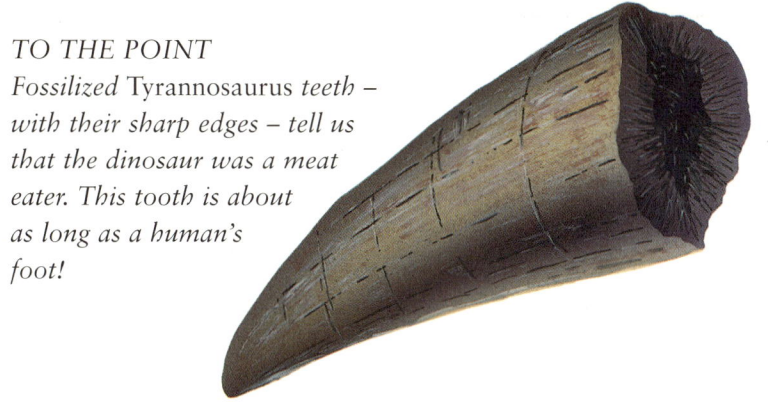

TO THE POINT
Fossilized Tyrannosaurus *teeth – with their sharp edges – tell us that the dinosaur was a meat eater. This tooth is about as long as a human's foot!*

Mantell recognized their similarity to the teeth of the iguana, a living reptile, and after much research he decided they must have belonged to some giant plant-eating reptile and he named the creature *Iguanodon*, meaning "iguana tooth". An English scientist called Richard Owen realized that these bones came from a group of reptiles that no longer existed and, in 1841, he gave these mysterious creatures a name – "dinosaurs".

Dinosaur fever spread to the United States, where in the late 19th century many discoveries were made. A large number of these were made by Edward Drinker Cope and Othniel Charles Marsh. Another famous dinosaur hunter was Roy Chapman Andrews, who led a fossil hunt to the Gobi Desert in the 1920s. The expedition made many important dinosaur discoveries, including dinosaur eggs and the skeletons of such dinosaurs as *Oviraptor* and *Protoceratops*.

- **Naming a dinosaur**
  - When the remains of a new dinosaur are discovered, even if there are just a few bones, that creature is given a name. This name is usually made up of Latin or Greek words and may refer to some feature of the animal, or to its discoverer or to where it was found.
  - The name *Deinonychus* means "terrible claw" and refers to the fearsome claws on each foot of this dinosaur.
  - The plant eater *Riojasaurus* was named after La Rioja in Argentina where it was found.
  - *Othnielia*, a hypsilophodont, was named after its discoverer – Professor Othniel Marsh, an American fossil hunter of the 19th century.

- **New finds**
  - New discoveries are still being made and not all are found by scientific expeditions. In 1999 a young Madagascan boy led scientists to an extraordinary collection of fossils on the island, including some of the earliest dinosaurs discovered.

INTRODUCTION TO

DINOSAUR LIFE STYLES

Just like animals today, dinosaurs spent much of their time finding food to eat. By looking at dinosaur teeth and jaw structure it is possible to find out whether they were plant eaters or meat eaters. It was not easy being either kind of dinosaur. Plant eaters always had a plentiful supply of food but had to eat a large amount to get enough nourishment to keep them alive. One good meal might last a meat eater several days – but it had to catch the meal first!

SAUROPODS

The biggest dinosaurs of all, the sauropods (see pages 28–31), were plant eaters. These giants probably had to eat as much as a tonne (1 ton) of plant food every day (about 100 large Christmas turkeys!). Their size and their long neck allowed them to feed on the leaves at the tops of trees that smaller dinosaurs could not stretch up to.

TREE–TOP MEALS
Only the long-necked sauropods could reach the fresh young leaves at the very tops of trees. Other plant eaters had to feed at lower levels, so the sauropods had no competition.

Allosaurus used its ferociously sharp teeth and very strong jaws to rip and tear at the flesh of predators.

PREDATORS

Like hunters today, meat-eating dinosaurs had to chase and kill their prey. Large predators, such as tyrannosaurs, were equipped with razor-sharp teeth and strong jaws to help them kill. Smaller hunters such as fast-running *Velociraptor* may have hunted in packs, just like hunting dogs today. Together they could have brought down dinosaurs much larger than themselves.

Plant eaters had different ways of defending themselves. Few hunters dared to attack the giant sauropods. Armoured dinosaurs, such as ankylosaurs, were covered with spikes and bony plates which protected them. If attacked, an armoured dinosaur could lash out at its enemy with the bony spike at the end of its tail.

FISH HOOK
The 30-centimetre (12-inch) curved claws on each hand may have helped Baryonyx *catch its slippery prey.*

Dinosaur dinners
- A few dinosaurs probably had specialized diets. A dinosaur named *Baryonyx*, found in England, may have fed largely on fish. It had long jaws and a large number of teeth – ideal for seizing fish.
- Sauropods' slender teeth were ideal for stripping the leaves from the branches but not so suitable for chewing. Instead the dinosaur probably swallowed a number of stones which remained in the stomach and ground the food down once swallowed – many birds today swallow small stones for the same purpose.
- Plant eaters, such as hadrosaurs, could chop tough leaves from trees with their flat toothless beak at the front of the jaws. They then ground the food down with their rows of closely packed teeth farther back. With the help of these teeth and powerful jaw muscles, hadrosaurs could tackle such tough plant material as conifer needles and bark.

DINOSAUR LIFE STYLES

DINOSAUR FAMILIES

Like most reptiles that are alive today, dinosaurs are believed to have laid eggs. For a long time dinosaur experts thought that dinosaurs simply buried their eggs in the ground and left them to hatch by themselves, just like turtles do today. Discoveries suggest that some kinds of dinosaurs may have tried to be good parents to their young.

MAIASAURA
One of the most important discoveries was of a number of eggs and nests in Montana in western North America. These belonged to a duckbill dinosaur given the name of *Maiasaura*, meaning "good mother lizard". *Maiasaura* is thought to have nested in colonies (as many as 40 nests were found in one small area) and it probably used the same nests year after year. Each nest was a hollow in the earth, lined with plants and measuring about 2 to 3 metres (about 7 to 10 feet) across.

A GOOD MOTHER
Maiasaura was a member of the duckbill family, a group of large, plant-eating dinosaurs common during the Late Cretaceous. These dinosaurs made nests for their eggs. At the start of the breeding season, each female would have made a shallow hollow in the ground before carefully depositing her eggs.

The nests were carefully spaced apart, leaving enough room for the parent dinosaurs to lie beside each nest guarding their babies. Each nest contained as many as 20 to 25 eggs arranged in layers in neat circles. The whole clutch was covered with sand and leaves to keep the eggs warm while they incubated.

PROTOCERATOPS
Nests and eggs belonging to Protoceratops *have been found in the Gobi Desert in Asia. Each nest was a shallow hole in the ground and contained up to 20 eggs arranged in circles.*

Family secrets
- So far, research suggests that, like birds today, some baby dinosaurs were able to walk around and fend for themselves right away, while others were born in a weaker state and needed the care of their parents for a time. More and more is being discovered about dinosaurs and their eggs and we may learn that they had many different ways of caring for their young – just like animals today.
- Fossils of baby *Maiasaura* dinosaurs show that they measured about 35 centimetres (14 inches) long when hatched. The babies were probably too small and weak to manage by themselves and would have depended on their parents for food and protection. If these dinosaurs did nest in colonies they may have shared the care of their young with some adults – perhaps some dinosaurs remained on guard while others went to feed.

INTRODUCTION TO
MEAT-EATING DINOSAURS

The ceratosaur group includes about 20 species of predatory dinosaur which were the first of the theropods, or flesh-eating dinosaurs. The earliest ceratosaur fossils date from about 225 million years ago, in the Late Triassic, and the group survived until the Late Cretaceous.

"MEAT-EATING BULL"

Carnotaurus means "meat-eating bull" and this dinosaur did have a large bull-like head, with sharp horns. Its arms were even shorter than those of most ceratosaurs. *Carnotaurus* lived in Argentina during the Late Cretaceous and grew to a length of about 7.5 metres (25 feet). Fossilized skin impressions show that its body may have been covered with small cone-shaped plates.

A TINY DINOSAUR
At only about 60 centimetres (24 inches) long, the tiny, bird-like Compsognathus *was one of the smallest of all dinosaurs. A speedy dinosaur, it probably preyed on small reptiles such as lizards, which it caught with its small sharp teeth and clawed hands. It lived in Europe about 155 to 145 million years ago, during the Late Jurassic.*

Carnotaurus

Despite its threatening appearance, *Carnotaurus* had a weak lower jaw, compared to other carnivorous dinosaurs. Scientists suspect that it may have often fed on carrion, creatures that were already dead, more often than killing its own prey.

TRIASSIC CANNIBAL

The *Coelophysis* was a small slender creature, about 2.8 metres (9 feet) long, with a pointed head and a long neck. Its jaws were lined with a large number of small, jagged-edged teeth. It probably preyed on creatures such as small reptiles and fish and may have even eaten its own kind. Some *Coelophysis* skeletons have contained the bones of young individuals. At first some experts believed that this meant that they gave birth to live young instead of laying eggs. Now most scientists agree that *Coelophysis* was probably a cannibal.

Coelophysis

Ceratosaur facts
- One of the most extraordinary dinosaur finds was made in New Mexico where the bones of hundreds of *Coelophysis* dinosaurs were discovered buried together. The large number of skeletons found in one place suggests that this dinosaur probably moved in herds. *Coelophysis* lived in the Late Triassic and was one of the earliest dinosaurs known.
- Ceratosaurs differed dramatically in size, ranging from the chicken-sized *Compsognathus* to creatures such as the terrifying 7-metre (23-feet) long *Ceratosaurus*. They walked upright on their two back legs and had short arms. Like all theropods they had hollow bones, which were light but strong, and several kinds of ceratosaur had horns or crests on their heads. Ceratosaurs, like other theropods, belonged to the saurischian dinosaur group.

MEAT-EATING DINOSAURS

TETANURANS

Tetanurans were giant meat-eating dinosaurs which lived during the Jurassic and Cretaceous. Tetanurans are also known as "stiff tails" because of the special vertebrae (backbones) in the tail which helped to keep them rigid. Typically, tetanurans had a bulky body and short arms with strong clawed fingers.

They walked upright on their powerfully-muscled back legs, using their long tail to help balance the weight of its body.

PACK HUNTER
Allosaurus was one of the most common of the tetanurans. It lived in North America during the Late Jurassic and Early Cretaceous and grew up to 12 metres (39 feet) long. Herds of sauropods lived alongside this predator. Although Allosaurus could not have tackled these giants on its own, it may have worked in packs to single out one from the herd and bring it down. Fossil trackways of the two kinds of dinosaur show evidence of this. Tracks also suggest that Allosaurus may have been able to move at speeds of more than 30 kilometres per hour (19 miles per hour) as it chased its prey. On its head this dinosaur had two short horns just above the eyes. These may have helped Allosaurus frighten off rivals and could have been used in headbutting battles.

GASOSAURUS
Also discovered in China was Gasosaurus. This dinosaur was small compared to most tetanurans, measuring only about 4 metres (13 feet) long. It lived during the Late Jurassic and probably hunted in wolf-like packs, like its relatives.

CHINESE DINOSAUR
Yangchuanosaurus lived in China during the Late Jurassic. It grew up to 10 metres (33 feet) long and had a massive tail that was about half of its length. Its skull measured up to a metre (3 feet) in length and there was a bony knob on its nose. This dinosaur hunted in packs and would have attacked with its large serrated teeth and sharp clawed fingers.

Big and dangerous
- These fierce creatures included one of the largest of all predatory dinosaurs, the recently discovered *Gigantosaurus*. This dinosaur, whose fossils were discovered in South America in 1993, grew up to 13 metres (43 feet) long and probably weighed as much as 8 tonnes (8 tons).
- Another recent discovery thought to belong to this group was *Carcharodontosaurus*, which was found in the North African desert in 1996. This giant may have been as big as 8 metres (26 feet) long. At 1.6 metres (5 feet) long, its skull was larger even than that of *Tyrannosaurus* and it had vicious, dagger-like teeth, for ripping and tearing the flesh of its prey, each measuring 12 centimetres (5 inches) – the size of a small banana!

MEAT-EATING DINOSAURS

MANIRAPTORANS

This group contains a number of lightly built dinosaurs which are thought to be closely related to birds. In fact many experts believe that these dinosaurs were the ancestors of birds.

Maniraptorans lived from the Late Jurassic through the Cretaceous and included such hunters as *Dromaeosaurus*. These dinosaurs were less than 2 metres (7 feet) long but are thought to have hunted in packs and preyed on plant eaters much larger than themselves. Also included in this group were the tröodontid dinosaurs such as *Tröodon* and *Saurornithoides*. These dinosaurs were up to 2 metres (7 feet) long, with slender legs. Their long jaws were filled with sharp, saw-edged teeth and their long-fingered hands bore sharp claws, ideal for seizing prey. Like other carnivorous dinosaurs, Maniraptorans belonged to the saurischian dinosaur group.

"TERRIBLE CLAW"
With its 12-centimetre (5 inch) claws on the second toe of each foot, Deinonychus was a particularly fierce predator – the name Deinonychus means "terrible claw". Once close enough to its prey the dinosaur could balance on one leg and slash at its victim with the claw on its other foot. This dinosaur lived in North America during the Early Cretaceous and grew up to about 4 metres (13 feet) long.

TRÖODON
The name of this dinosaur means "wounding tooth" and it did indeed have powerful teeth, with jagged edges like a steak knife, in its long jaws. Tröodon lived in western North America about 75 to 70 million years ago during the Late Cretaceous. It grew to about 1.75 metres (6 feet) long and possibly weighed about 50 kilograms (110 pounds).

A FEROCIOUS BATTLE
One of the most extraordinary fossils ever found was discovered in Mongolia. It shows the carnivorous dinosaur Velociraptor in the act of attacking a horned dinosaur named Protoceratops. The two must have been killed, perhaps by a sudden sandstorm, in the middle of their battle, with Velociraptor's head trapped in the jaws of Protoceratops. A fierce hunter, Velociraptor was only about 1.8 metres (6 feet) long. It lived in the Late Cretaceous in China.

Secrets of its success
- All maniraptorans were hunters and could run fast on their two back legs.
- Although their front limbs were small, they were not useless like those of tyrannosaurs. Their wrist joints were extremely flexible which helped them to seize prey, and most had long sharp claws.
- In relation to their body size, tröodontids are thought to have the largest brains of any dinosaur. They probably had excellent sight and hearing too.
- *Dromaeosaurus* had a special weapon – a killing claw on the second toe of each foot. This claw was normally held back off the ground to prevent it from becoming blunt as it dragged on the ground, but could be swiftly moved forward when the dinosaur went on the attack.

ORNITHOMIMIDS

Ornithomimids, or ostrich dinosaurs, get their name from their amazing similarity to ostriches – the large flightless birds that live in southern Africa today. Like ostriches, ornithomimid dinosaurs had long back legs, long slender necks and small heads and were probably fast runners – ostriches hold the speed record for land birds today.

The ostrich dinosaurs lived in Asia and North America during the Late Cretaceous period. They grew to about 4 metres (13 feet) long – twice the size of an ostrich. Like all carnivorous dinosaurs, it belonged to the saurischian group of dinosaurs.

THE BIGGEST ORNITHOMIMID

Gallimimus *lived in the Mongolian area of Asia during the Late Cretaceous period. The largest ostrich dinosaur known,* Gallimimus *grew to more than 4 metres (13 feet) long and probably weighed about 150 kilograms (330 pounds). Like its relatives, it had long, slender legs and shorter arms with three-clawed fingers on each hand. Its long tail was held straight out behind it and would have helped to balance the weight of the front of the body when it ran.*

"OSTRICH MIMIC"
Struthiomimus, which means "ostrich mimic" lived in North America during the Late Cretaceous. It grew to about 3.5 metres (11 feet) long and had the long slender legs and small head typical of its relatives. Using its toothless beak, *Struthiomimus* would have snapped up food such as small lizards and insects.

A GOOD MOTHER
Another Mongolian ornithomimid was *Oviraptor,* a 2-metre (7-feet) long dinosaur which lived in the Late Cretaceous. Its name means "egg thief", a name mistakenly given to the dinosaur when scientists found a fossilized skeleton with eggs thought to belong to another dinosaur. Now another *Oviraptor* fossil has been found, apparently sitting on its clutch of 15 large eggs with its legs tucked behind its body just like a brooding bird today.

Long, lean and fast
- With its light build and long legs, the ostrich dinosaur may have run at speeds of up to 65 kilometres an hour (40 miles per hour) – as fast as many professional sprinters – as it searched for small lizards, small mammals and insects to eat.
- The ostrich dinosaur probably fed on leaves and berries and sometimes the eggs of other dinosaurs using its beak-like mouth to pick at the fruit or eggs.
- The ostrich dinosaur had no teeth, so it had to snatch food in its toothless beak at the front of its jaws.
- Skulls that have been discovered show that it had a large brain – so ostrich dinosaurs were probably intelligent. Their large eye sockets suggest that they also had very good eyesight.
- Ostrich dinosaurs probably had scaly skin without feathers – unlike their modern lookalike.

25

Tyrannosaurs

Huge and ferocious, the tyrannosaurs are the largest land predators the world has ever known. These dagger-toothed hunters roamed North America and Asia during the Late Cretaceous, preying on plant eaters such as duckbilled dinosaurs.

Typically a tyrannosaur had strong back legs with tiny arms and strong deep jaws, equipped with saw-edged teeth. It ran upright on its back legs, holding its long deep tail out behind it to balance the weight of the front of its body and massive head. Dinosaur experts have tried to find out if the tyrannosaur was a hunter or not. Now they believe that the structure of their legs show that tyrannosaurs could have moved fast, something that would not have been necessary for creatures that lived on carrion (animals that were already dead and did not need to be killed by the tyrannosaur).

TARBOSAURUS
At 14 metres (46 feet) long, the giant Tarbosaurus *terrorized plant eaters in Central Asia during the Late Cretaceous. It was similar in structure to* Tyrannosaurus, *but had a less bulky body and a longer skull. Like its relative, it would have patrolled the forests, hunting duckbills and other dinosaurs and tearing them apart with its massive teeth.*

Its extraordinarily powerful teeth also suggest an animal that had to kill its food. Even so, tyrannosaurs probably ate carrion when they came across it – just like lions do today. Tyrannosaurs belonged to the saurischian group of dinosaurs.

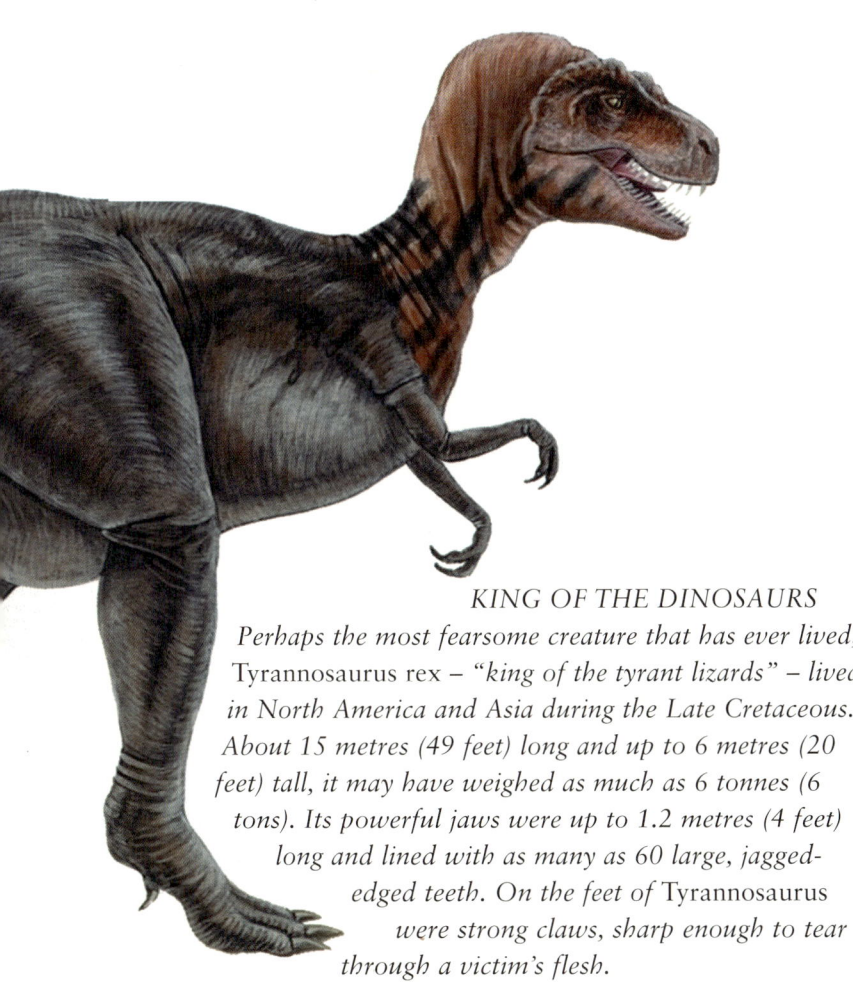

KING OF THE DINOSAURS
Perhaps the most fearsome creature that has ever lived, Tyrannosaurus rex – "king of the tyrant lizards" – lived in North America and Asia during the Late Cretaceous. About 15 metres (49 feet) long and up to 6 metres (20 feet) tall, it may have weighed as much as 6 tonnes (6 tons). Its powerful jaws were up to 1.2 metres (4 feet) long and lined with as many as 60 large, jagged-edged teeth. On the feet of Tyrannosaurus were strong claws, sharp enough to tear through a victim's flesh.

Tyrannosaur trivia
- The short arms and two-fingered hands of a tyrannosaur were amazingly small compared to the rest of the animal. They would have been of little use for catching prey and were too small to pass food to the mouth. Some dinosaur experts have suggested that their only use may have been to help the tyrannosaur lift itself up off the ground after sleeping.
- Some dinosaur experts have suggested that these huge creatures were too big to chase and catch prey – their weight might have just tipped them over – and that instead they scavenged for all their food, eating carrion. Not all experts agree with this theory.
- Some of *Tyrannosaurus rex*'s horrific teeth were 15 centimetres (6 inches) long and so strong that they could bite into a victim's flesh and even crunch its bones!

INTRODUCTION TO

PLANT-EATING DINOSAURS

Among the earliest known dinosaurs, plant-eating prosauropods lived from the Late Triassic until the end of the Early Jurassic. Experts believe that they were not an early form of sauropod (see page 30–31) but a separate, related group. However, like sauropods, they were saurischian dinosaurs. Typically, a prosauropod had a bulky body, fairly long neck, small head and long tail. The back legs were large and thick with five-toed feet; the front legs were more slender. The hands bore curving thumb claws.

PLATEOSAURUS
Plateosaurus *is thought to have been one of the most common dinosaurs living in Europe in the Late Triassic. About 8 metres (26 feet) long, it had a long neck, small head and large, five-fingered hands. Its back legs were longer than its front legs and it may have been able to rear up on its back legs and feed on the leaves of tall conifers and cycads. Dozens of skeletons of this dinosaur were found in one area of Germany, suggesting that* Plateosaurus *may have lived in large herds.*

RIOJASAURUS
Fossils of **Riojasaurus**, *a melanosaurid dating from the Late Triassic and Early Jurassic, have been found in Argentina in South America. This dinosaur, which grew to about 11 metres (36 feet) long, had a heavy body, bulky legs and a long neck and tail. It probably moved slowly on all fours and was unable to rear up on its back legs.*

The teeth of prosauropods were mainly leaf-shaped with ridged edges – not the typical shape for a plant eater. Some experts have wondered if these creatures could have been flesh eaters but they were not built for speed and did not have the strong jaws and vicious claws of most predators.

Most experts now agree that they probably did eat plant material, tearing and shredding leaves from the trees with their weak teeth, and that they may have swallowed small stones to help grind down tough food inside the gut.

Plateosaurids, melanosaurids and anchisaurids

- Three of the best known groups of prosauropods were the large, heavily built plateosaurids and melanosaurids and the smaller, lighter anchisaurids. The anchisaurids were only about 2 to 3 metres (6 to 10 feet) long and their slender build would have allowed them to walk on two legs some of the time. The larger plateosaurids grew up to 8 metres (26 feet) long and had bulky bodies and long tails. They may have been too big to walk upright but could have reared up to feed on high plants.

Melanosaurids included the biggest of the prosauropods, up to 12 metres (39 feet) long, and would have been too heavy to stand on their back legs.

PLANT-EATING DINOSAURS

SAUROPODS

Sauropods were the largest land animals that have ever lived. Even the smallest species of this group of plant-eating giants were at least 15 metres (49 feet) long and some of the most recent discoveries have measured more than 35 metres (115 feet).

Sauropods belonged to the saurischian group of dinosaurs. Typically, they had a small head, long neck with tail and very, thick heavy legs.

Camarasaurs were smaller than sauropods, such as brachiosaurs and diplodocids, and had shorter tails and larger skulls. One of the most common was *Camarasaurus* which probably lived in herds in western North America.

MIGHTY PLANT EATER
Camarasaurus lived in western North America in the Late Jurassic period. It measured up to 18 metres (59 feet) long – the same as four or five average cars parked end to end! It may have weighed as much as 20 tonnes (20 tons). Large herds of these giants would have wandered together, feeding on plants such as conifers and horse-tails.

Biggest of all the sauropods were the brachiosaurs. A typical brachiosaur had a small head and long neck, like other sauropods. But the brachiosaur had longer front legs than back legs so that its body sloped down towards its tail – like a giraffe. These amazing creatures lived in North America, Europe and Africa during the Jurassic and early Cretaceous.

For all sauropods their best defence was their size. If a sauropod was attacked, it could rear up briefly, bringing its massive feet down on its attacker, or it could lash at its enemy with its long whip-like tail.

BRACHIOSAURUS
One of the best known of all dinosaurs, Brachiosaurus *lived in North America during the Late Jurassic. At about 23 metres (75 feet) long, this dinosaur was as long as six family cars parked end to end. It may have weighed more than 80 tonnes (80 tons) – about the same as 12 African elephants.*

Special features
- One important feature of sauropods was that the vertebrae (the backbones) were partly hollow. This helped to make the animal lighter while still keeping it strong. This feature is more extreme in later sauropods.
- The long neck of a typical sauropod meant that its head, and therefore its brain, was a long way from its heart. Its heart must have been large and powerful and would have had to work very hard to pump blood all the way up the neck to the brain.

New discoveries
- In 1999 a new sauropod was identified that was discovered in the Sahara Desert in Africa a couple of years before. Named *Jobara* after "Jobar", a creature in local legends, this sauropod is thought to have been about 18 metres (60 feet) tall.

BONEHEADED DINOSAURS

These plant-eating dinosaurs lived in the Early to Late Cretaceous in North America, Asia and Europe. They were small to medium sized, ranging from 1 to 4.5 metres (3 to 15 feet) long, and walked upright on two legs. Their heavy tails helped to balance the body. Their arms were much shorter than their legs and they had five fingers.

BONEHEAD FAMILIES
Boneheaded dinosaurs, or boneheads, are best known for their dome-shaped skulls. The dome is actually a solid lump of bone.

THE LARGEST BONEHEAD
The largest known bonehead at about 4.5 metres (15 feet) long, Pachycephalosaurus lived in North America during the Late Cretaceous.

The bony dome on its head was as much as 25 centimetres (10 inches) thick. This bonehead survived longer than any others of its family, becoming extinct right at the end of the Cretaceous.

There were two families of boneheads – the pachycephalosaurs and the homalocephalids. The pachycephalosaurs had large domes on their heads, sometimes ringed with bony spikes and knobs. Males probably had bigger domes than females and the domes became larger as they grew older.

The bones of the Homalocephalid's skull were extra thick and the head was covered with knobs of bone. They lived in Asia during the Late Cretaceous.

BATTLING BONEHEAD
Stegoceras *lived in North America and China during the Late Cretaceous period and measured up to 2 metres (7 feet) long. When it charged it would have held its head down and kept its neck, body and tail in a straight line, like a battering ram. Its vertebrae were specially strengthened to help protect against damage to the back during head-clashing battles.*

- **Head-bangers**
- Dinosaur experts believe that, like certain kinds of goats and sheep, the boneheads may have been herding animals and taken part in headbutting battles. The battles probably took place during the breeding season when rival males fought to win females. With heads lowered and tails held straight out behind they charged one another, crashing their heads together. The thick dome of bone would have taken much of the impact and protected the animal's brain.
- *Homalocephale*, a typical member of the Homalocephalids family, had very wide hips and some experts have suggested that this was because they gave birth to live young instead of laying eggs. Most now believe that it is more likely that the wide hips helped to cushion some of the impact during the dinosaurs' headbashing battles.

PLANT-EATING DINOSAURS

Fabrosaurs and Hypsilophodonts

Fabrosaurs were small, plant-eating dinosaurs which were most common in the Early Jurassic. Fossils have been found in southern Africa and in China. These dinosaurs looked similar to lizards but walked upright on their long back legs. Lightly built and speedy, fabrosaurs such as *Lesothosaurus* could run long distances in search of plants to eat.

LESOTHOSAURUS
This lizard-like dinosaur lived in Africa in the Early Jurassic. It was about 1 metre (3 feet) long and ran fast on its slender back legs. It had a small head, large eyes and pointed teeth.

A FAST MOVER
Hypsilophodon lived in Europe and North America in the Late Cretaceous. It was a small dinosaur and measured about 1.5 metres (5 feet) long. Its name means "high ridge tooth" and comes from its tall grooved teeth towards the back of its jaws. These were used for chewing, while the toothless beak at the front of the jaws was ideal for chopping leaves from plants. A number of well-preserved skeletons of *Hypsilophodon* were found in the Isle of Wight, off the south coast of England. These show that it was slender and lightly built with long thin foot bones like a gazelle – an ideal body structure for a fast runner.

HYPSILOPHODONTS

Hypsilophodonts had a similar way of life to fabrosaurs and started to become common around the time fabrosaurs became extinct. Like deer today, hypsilophodonts were fast-running plant eaters which may have lived in herds. They would have been constantly on the alert for predators and if threatened would have relied on their speed for protection.

These small to medium-sized dinosaurs ranged from 3 to 5 metres (10 to 16 feet) long. They lived from the Middle Jurassic to the end of the Cretaceous and fossils have been found in North America, Europe, China, Australia and Antarctica.

Fabrosaurs and hypsilophodonts belonged to the ornithischian group of dinosaurs.

New finds
- Hypsilophodont nests have been discovered in Montana, USA, with the remains of eggs and young dinosaurs. The eggs were carefully arranged in circles, with tips pointing downwards into the earth. When they hatched, the young clambered out through the top half of the egg.
- When the dinosaur *Hypsilophodon* was first discovered in the 19th century, experts thought it was similar in structure to the modern tree kangaroo. They believed that it lived in trees holding on with its tail and its bird-like feet. In fact, experts now agree that *Hypsilophodon* was a fast-running land animal and not a tree-dweller.
- Like deer today, hypsilophodonts were fast-running plant eaters which may have lived in herds. They would have been constantly on the alert for predators and if they were threatened would have relied on their speed for protection.

PLANT-EATING DINOSAURS

IGUANODONTS

Iguanodonts were large plant-eating dinosaurs which could be up to 9 metres (30 feet) long. Found in North America, Europe, Africa, Asia and Australia, they first appeared in the Late Jurassic and lived until the Late Cretaceous.

Iguanodon may have walked on two legs or on all fours.

STEGOSAUR BUILD
Typically, iguanodonts had stocky bodies and heavy legs. They probably spent much of their time on all fours but they could have reared up on their back legs to feed on taller plants.

Stiff tail

"IGUANA TOOTH"
Iguanodon *lived in Europe, Asia, North America and Africa in the Early Cretaceous and grew to about 9 metres (30 feet) long. It may have moved in herds which wandered slowly through forests, feeding on plants.* Iguanodon *was only the second dinosaur to be discovered and named. Nineteenth-century fossil hunter Gideon Mantell who discovered some bones and teeth gave it the name* Iguanodon, *which means "iguana tooth", because he thought its teeth looked like those of iguana lizards.*

The head was long, rather like that of a horse, and the jaws ended in a strong toothless beak. Strong teeth farther back in the jaws were used for chewing. Like many plant-eating dinosaurs, iguanodonts had cheek pouches so that food did not fall out of the mouth as they chewed – most reptiles do not have cheek pouches and tend to swallow their food rather than chew it. The back legs of the iguanodonts were longer and heavier than their front legs and their feet bore three toes, each tipped with hoof-like claws.

Cheek pouch

Spiked thumb

Flexible fifth finger

Claws on back feet

An Amazing Hand
- *Iguanodon* had incredibly specialized and useful hands. Each hand had a strong spike instead of a thumb. This made a powerful weapon for use against enemies. The three middle fingers of the hand ended in hoof-shaped claws, while the fifth finger could be moved across the palm and used for holding food.
- When the first reconstruction of *Iguanodon* was done in 1825, no one knew where the spike (now known to be on the hand) belonged. Thinking it was a horn, these early experts placed the spike on the animal's snout.

The body warmer
- *Ouranosaurus* had a large sail-like structure on its back, made up of spines extending from the vertebrae and covered with skin. It could have been used to help the dinosaur control its body temperature. Blood in the sail could have been warmed when the dinosaur turned into the sun.

PLANT-EATING DINOSAURS

DUCKBILLED DINOSAURS

Named for the flat, toothless beak at the front of the jaws, duckbilled dinosaurs were perhaps the most common of all dinosaurs in the Late Cretaceous. The earliest members of the family lived in Asia, but the group soon spread to North and South America and to Europe.

PARASAUROLOPHUS
This duckbill lived in western North America in the Late Cretaceous period and was about 10 metres (33 feet) long. On its head was a long, backward-pointing crest which was up to 2 metres (7 feet) long. *Parasaurolophus* had a small notch in its backbone and its crest may have fitted neatly into this when it held its head up.

CORYTHOSAURUS
Corythosaurus was about 9 metres (30 feet) long and lived in North America.

DUCKBILL PLANT EATERS

Duckbills were medium to large animals. They grew up to about 13 metres (43 feet) long and had a heavy body and back legs which were longer than the front legs. They probably spent much of their time on all fours but may have been able to rear up onto their back legs, using their deep tails to help keep balance. Duckbills were plant eaters and had a lot of teeth farther back in the mouth for chewing tough food. As old teeth became worn and fell out, new teeth took their place. One reason for the success of this particular group of dinosaurs was that by the time they evolved flowering plants had spread over the world and plant food was more plentiful than ever before.

LAMBEOSAURUS
This dinosaur also lived in western North America and was about 9 metres (30 feet) long. On its head was a hollow, forward-pointing crest and a solid bony spike that pointed backwards.

Duckbill groups
- There were two groups of duckbills – the hadrosaurines and lambeosaurines.
- The hadrosaurines had flat heads, some with solid, bony crests on the top.
- The typical lambeosaurine had a more dome-shaped head, with a hollow crest. These crests varied in shape and may have made a chamber to make the dinosaurs' calls louder.
- Duckbills lived in herds and their calls could have helped them to keep in touch and warn each other of danger.

Cool crest
- *Corythosaurus* had a large fan-like crest, standing about 30 centimetres (12 inches) high, on top of its head. Inside the crest was a complex maze of hollow tubes, which may have helped the dinosaur make loud sounds and communicate with the others in its herd.
- Some experts think the tubes may have been a cooling system to help the animal cool down if it overheated.

What are Stegosaurs?

As large, plant-eating dinosaurs, stegosaurs are best known for the double rows of bony plates that ran along their backbones. These creatures lived from the mid Jurassic to the Late Cretaceous in North America, Europe, Africa and Asia and ranged from about 3 to 9 metres (10 to 30 feet) long. They belonged to the ornithischian group of dinosaurs.

Stegosaurs are thought to have lived in large herds, spending much of their time browsing on low plants.

THE BIGGEST STEGOSAUR
Stegosaurus *lived in western North America during the Late Jurassic and it is the largest known stegosaur.* It was up to 9 metres (30 feet) long and probably weighed as much as 2 tonnes (2 tons). The plates on its back were shaped like arrowheads and some stood up to 60 centimetres (24 inches) high. Stegosaurus's skull, however, was tiny – only about 40 centimetres (16 inches) long – and its brain was only the size of a walnut.

KENTROSAURUS
An African stegosaur, Kentrosaurus *was about 5 metres (16 feet) long. The bony plates on its back were narrower than those of* Stegosaurus *and towards the tail became sharp spikes. A pair of spikes also stuck out of its sides at the hips – these would have helped to protect it from enemies.*

STEGOSAUR DATA

They walked on four legs and were probably quite slow moving. A typical stegosaur had a large body, extremely small head and a deep tail equipped with sharp bony spikes. If attacked, it could have used its spiked tail to fend off the predator. The shape and pattern of the plates and spines on the back differed in each species of stegosaur.

CHINESE STEGOSAUR
Tuojiangosaurus *lived in China in the Late Jurassic and was up to 7 metres (23 feet) long. On its back were 15 pairs of bony plates. Two pairs of spikes armed its tail. Like* Stegosaurus, *it had a small, narrow head.*

Hot plates
- None of the stegosaur skeletons that have been found have had the back plates attached to the body and palaeontologists have argued about their purpose and arrangement. Some say that the plates lay flat on the body for protection from attack. Others think that they may have helped the animals to recognize each other or find mates.
- Many experts now believe that the plates stood upright, arranged either in pairs or two alternating rows, and that they may have helped the dinosaur control its body temperature. The plates may have been covered in a layer of skin rich in blood vessels. If the dinosaur was cold, it could have stood with the plates facing the sun. The blood would then have been warmed through the skin. If the dinosaur became too warm it could have turned into the wind so the blood cooled as it passed over the plates.

PLANT-EATING DINOSAURS

ARMOURED DINOSAURS

These extraordinary creatures had their own body armour to protect them from attackers. Flat bony plates covered the neck, back and sides and many of these plates were also covered with spikes and knobs.

FULL ARMOUR PLATING
North American armoured dinosaur, Euoplocephalus *lived in the Late Cretaceous. It grew up to 5.5 metres (18 feet) long and weighed as much as 2 tonnes (2 tons). Large bony studs covered the bony plates on its body and spikes stuck out from the base of the tail and shoulders for further protection. The skull was heavy and covered with extra pieces of bone and bony coverings shielded the eyelids from damage. Only its belly was vulnerable to attack.*

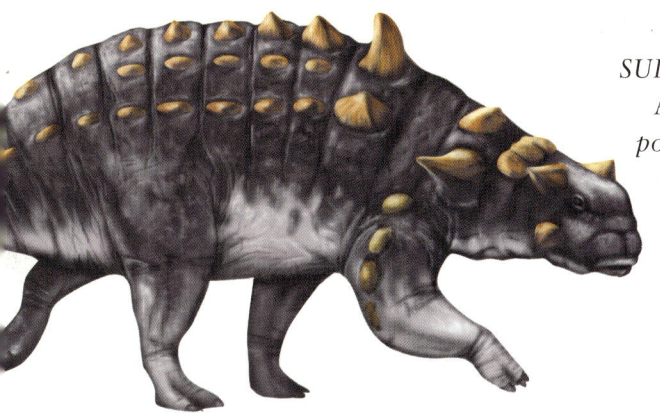

SUIT OF ARMOUR
Ankylosaurus had powerful legs and a heavily armoured body and skull.

NODOSAURS AND ANKYLOSAURS

There were two families of armoured dinosaurs – the nodosaurs and the ankylosaurs. Both were ornithischians. The nodosaurs came first in the Late Jurassic or Early Cretaceous. Most lived in North America, Europe and Asia. Ankylosaurs evolved in the Cretaceous and largely took over from nodosaurs.

All were plant eaters and probably fed mostly on smaller plants or the lower leaves of trees – up to about 2 metres (7 feet) off the ground. Nodosaurs had a long narrow snout and could have chosen certain plants to eat. Ankylosaurs had a much broader head and probably just snapped up any plants they came across with the wide, toothless beak at the front of the jaws.

Living tanks

- Ankylosaurs were probably better armoured than nodosaurs, with bony plates and spikes on the head and bony shutters that came down over the eyes.
- Ankylosaurs had a special weapon – a ball of bone at the end of the tail which acted like a club. The dinosaur could swing this club at an attacker and even break the leg of a mighty tyrannosaur. The hip muscles were extra powerful to help the dinosaur swing this heavy tail club from side to side.
- The club was made up of several large pieces of bone joined together and then joined to the tail bones. The tail was very strong to help support the weight of the bony club.
- Nodosaurs and ankylosaurs had short, sturdy legs to support their bulky armoured bodies and would have walked on all fours. They were probably slow movers and depended on their armour to protect them from predators.

PLANT-EATING DINOSAURS

PARROT DINOSAURS AND EARLY HORNED DINOSAURS

Parrot dinosaurs lived in the Early Cretaceous in parts of Asia and were the ancestors of horned dinosaurs. They get their name from the toothless beak at the front of the jaws – a beak similar to that of a parrot.

WALKING AND EATING
Parrot dinosaurs used their sharp beaks and strong jaws to crop plants, including the flowering plants that were then beginning to spread across the world. They were lighter than the horned dinosaurs so parrot dinosaurs could walk upright on their back legs and run to escape from enemies.

PARROT DINOSAUR
Psittacosaurus *lived in Asia in the Late Cretaceous. It grew up to 2.5 metres (8 feet) long and had the square-shaped skull and parrot-like beak typical of its family.*

On the sides of its head were a pair of horn-like bumps – an early version of the horns of the horned dinosaurs which came later.

MONGOLIAN DINOSAUR
This early horned dinosaur measured about 2.7 metres (9 feet) long and may have weighed as much 180 kilograms (396 pounds). It lived in Asia in the Late Cretaceous period. At the back of its large head was a broad bony neck frill and on its nose was a crest-like bump. The many skulls of this dinosaur discovered in Mongolia suggest that male Protoceratops *were larger and had much bigger nose bumps than females.*

Parrot dinosaurs walked on all fours when feeding on low plants. On their front limbs two of the fingers were extremely small, leaving them only three usable fingers.

Protoceratopsians, the first horned dinosaurs, also evolved in Asia in the Late Cretaceous period and spread to North America. They were smaller and lighter than later horned dinosaurs and could probably run on two legs when necessary. Parrot dinosaurs and horned dinosaurs were ornithischian dinosaurs.

• Strange eating habits
- Like some larger plant eaters, parrot dinosaurs may have swallowed small stones to help break down tough leaves – skeletons have been found with these stones, called gastroliths, inside the rib cage. As the food passed along the gut it would have been ground between the stones and so made easier to digest.

• A caring parent!
- Large numbers of *Protoceratops* remains have been discovered in Mongolia. When a number of eggs were also found in the area they were also thought to belong to *Protoceratops*. Fossil hunters found a skeleton of a carnivorous dinosaur on top of a nest of eggs believed to belong to *Protoceratops*. The hunter was named *Oviraptor*, meaning "egg stealer" and branded as a villain. Only recently have experts realized that in fact the eggs were *Oviraptor's* own and that it may have died protecting them. It was not an egg stealer at all but a caring parent!

PLANT-EATING DINOSAURS

LATER HORNED DINOSAURS

Huge herds of mighty horned dinosaurs, called ceratopsians, roamed western North America in the Late Cretaceous. They thrived for 20 million years until they became extinct with other dinosaurs at the end of the period. These great creatures were heavily armoured with large frill-like structures made of heavy bone growing out at the back of their heads and sharp horns on their snout. Their skin was thick and their legs and feet were large and heavy. Built for power not speed, they would have moved on all fours. They fed on leaves and other plant material, which they cropped with the sharp beak at the front of the jaws.

"THREE-HORNED FACE"
One of the largest and most common of the horned dinosaurs, Triceratops *was up to 9 metres (30 feet) long and weighed as much as 10 tonnes (11 tons). It had a short neck frill and three horns on its snout – the name* Triceratops *means "three-horned face". The long brow horns were up to 1 metre (3 feet) long.*

A HORNED ATTACK
Like Triceratops, Centrosaurus *had three horns on its snout – one long and two shorter ones above its eyes. Despite the huge bony frill behind its head,* Centrosaurus *had a flexible neck and could turn its head quickly to use its horns against attackers.*

CHARGING AHEAD

When in danger, a horned dinosaur may have lowered its mighty head and charged the enemy, rather like a rhinoceros. Even a tyrannosaur may have been alarmed at the sight of one of these living battering-rams hurtling towards it!

SPIKED NECK FRILL
The amazing neck frill of Styracosaurus *was ringed with large spikes, giving it a very threatening appearance. It also had a large straight horn on its nose which it could have used to defend itself.* Styracosaurus *lived in western North America in the Late Cretaceous and was about 5 metres (16 feet) long.*

- **Big-headed dinosaurs**
  - There were two groups of later horned dinosaurs – one group had short neck frills and the other much longer neck frills. These bony shields protected the head and neck area and made the dinosaurs very difficult for a predator to attack. The frills were often adorned with extra studs and spikes, making the dinosaur look even more fearsome.
- **Locking horns**
  - As well as using their horns against predators, ceratopsians may have also needed them in fights with rivals of their own kind. The dinosaurs lived in herds and, much like deer today, may have locked horns in battles over territory or mates. If predators threatened the herd, adult horned dinosaurs may have formed a protective circle, with young, weaker animals at the centre – just like some kinds of oxen do today.

INTRODUCTION TO

OTHER REPTILES

The first turtles lived 200 million years ago, in the Late Triassic, but looked remarkably similar to turtles of today. They had a hard shell protecting the back, bony plates covering the underside and a solid bony skull. Some could probably pull their head into the shell if attacked – just like turtles and tortoises today. Most fed on plants and had a hard beak at the front of the jaws for biting off their food.

AN EARLY CROCODILE
This ferocious-looking crocodile lived in North America in the Late Cretaceous. Few fossils have been found but its 2-metres-(7 feet-) long skull suggests that its total length was about 15 metres (49 feet). Like crocodiles today, Deinosuchus probably lay hidden in the water, waiting to ambush prey.

SEA TURTLE
Unlike most turtles, Archelon *did not have a heavy shell. Instead bony struts covered with a thick layer of skin, similar to that of the leatherback turtle of today, covered its back. It used its huge paddle-like limbs to push itself through the water – the front flippers were much larger than the back pair. Its jaws were weak and, like the leatherback, it may have fed mainly on soft jellyfish.* Archelon *was about 4 metres (13 feet) long and lived in the seas that covered parts of North America during the Late Cretaceous period.*

CROCODILE RELATIVES

True crocodiles first appeared in the Early Jurassic but there were some crocodile-like relatives as early as the Triassic. Early examples, such as *Terrestrisuchus* which lived in Europe, had longer legs than a true crocodile and may have fed mainly on insects. Later animals, such as *Deinosuchus*, had long jaws and short sprawling legs like crocodiles today. They also had an armour of bony plates set in the skin to protect the body. Most lived in rivers and swamps and preyed on animals that came close to the water's edge to drink.

- **Turtle skulls**
  - Like other early reptiles, turtles had a solid box-like skull with no openings except for the eyes and nostrils. Later reptiles, including dinosaurs, had openings called fenestrae in the skull. These lightened the weight and also provided attachment points for muscles, allowing more powerful jaw movements.
- **Crocodile facts**
  - Like dinosaurs, crocodiles belonged to the ruling reptiles. They are the only members of this group to survive today.
  - Another sea dweller was *Metriorhynchus*, an Early Jurassic crocodile, which had a fish-like fin on its tail for moving in water. It did not have the heavy bony plates which protected the bodies of most crocodiles because these would have made it too heavy to swim.
  - *Teleosaurus* lived in the sea and had very long narrow jaws, ideal for catching fish and squid.

OTHER REPTILES

Plesiosaurs and Pliosaurs

At the time of the dinosaurs, many kinds of marine reptiles lived in the sea. Some of the largest and most successful were the plesiosaurs. They had long flippers instead of limbs and moved through the water by beating their flippers up and down, rather like sea turtles and penguins do today. Although they spent most of their lives in the sea, plesiosaurs were air-breathing reptiles and had to surface regularly to breathe.

PLESIOSAUR GROUPS

There were four main groups of plesiosaurs, some with short necks and some with long necks. Those called plesiosaurids and cryptoclidids all had long necks and small heads. Their jaws were long and equipped with pointed teeth ideal for catching fish and squid. Elasmosaurs, which lived from the Late Jurassic to the Late Cretaceous, had an even longer neck. The fourth main group, the pliosaurs, had much shorter necks and large heavy heads, equipped with strong jaws.

GIANT PLIOSAUR
Kronosaurus is the largest pliosaur known and measured nearly 13 metres (43 feet) long. Its head alone measured more than 2.7 metres (9 feet) – about quarter of the length of its body. *Kronosaurus* lived in the Early Cretaceous in the seas that covered part of Australia. Its great size and its large, sharp teeth made this reptile the most powerful hunter of its time. It preyed on other plesiosaurs and ichthyosaurs as well as on fish and ammonites.

LONG-NECKED PLESIOSAUR
Elasmosaurus had an extraordinarily long neck. Its neck alone measured 8 metres (26 feet) of the reptile's total length of 14 metres (46 feet) and contained as many as 75 vertebrae or neck bones. Even a giraffe today has only seven neck bones, although each one is very long. The plesiosaur may have swum with its neck and head held above the water as it searched for prey.

Life underwater
- Plesiosaurs would have spent most of their life in the sea. But, like turtles today, they may have laid their eggs on land. They could have crawled up onto beaches, laid their eggs in pits in the sand and left them to hatch by themselves.
- Some plesiosaur fossils have been found with small stones in the stomach area. Perhaps the reptiles swallowed these to help them grind down their food or to give them extra weight and help them dive to greater depths.

Other marine animals
- During the Triassic period, reptiles called placodonts lived on land and water, feeding on shellfish.
- Nothosaurs may have lived rather like seals do today – catching food in water and spending some of their time on land. A typical nothosaur had a long body and tail and webbed feet to help power its swimming.

ICHTHYOSAURS

The name ichthyosaur means "fish lizard" and of all the marine reptiles at the time of the dinosaurs, ichthyosaurs were the best adapted to life in the sea. Even though they spent their whole lives in the water, ichthyosaurs were still air-breathing reptiles and had to come to the surface to breathe.

ICHTHYOSAUR LIFE

A typical ichthyosaur had a streamlined, torpedo-shaped body, similar to that of a dolphin, which was ideal for speedy swimming. It also had two pairs of flippers at the sides of the body, a large fin on the back and a fish-like tail. Instead of using flippers for movement, an ichthyosaur pushed itself through the water by moving its tail-fin from side to side, just like a shark does today. The side-fins helped the ichthyosaur change direction and balance its body as it swam. The nostrils were positioned high on its head, allowing the ichthyosaur to breathe without bringing its head far out of the water. Ichthyosaurs first lived in the Early Triassic and continued to thrive until the mid Cretaceous. They had strong jaws and sharp teeth and fed mainly on fish and squid. Many ichthyosaurs had large eyes and may have relied on sight for finding prey.

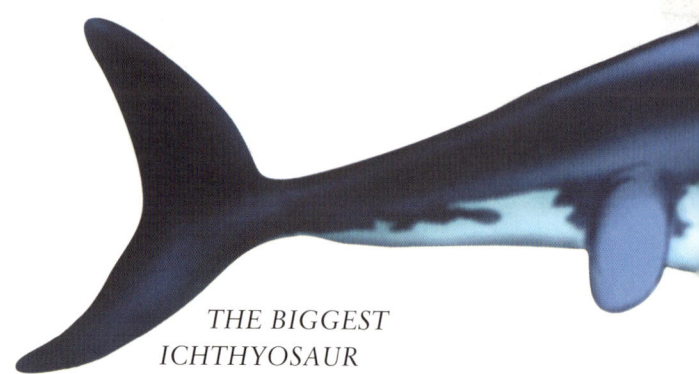

THE BIGGEST ICHTHYOSAUR
At 15 metres (49 feet) long, Shonisaurus was the largest ichthyosaur known. Its jaws were particularly long, with teeth only at the front. It had four long flippers of equal size – in most ichthyosaurs the front flippers were longer than the back ones. Shonisaurus lived during the Late Triassic and belonged to one of the earliest families of ichthyosaurs.

SPEEDY SWIMMER

Ichthyosaurus *lived from the Early Jurassic to Early Cretaceous in European seas. It grew to about 2 metres (7 feet) long and had a high fin on its back and a large tail-fin. A fast swimmer,* Ichthyosaurus *may have been able to move through the water at speeds of up to 40 kilometres an hour (25 miles per hour). Fossils of this ichthyosaur have been found that appear to show the reptile in the act of giving birth, with the young halfway out of the mother's body.*

Water babies

- The fish-like shape and weak flippers of ichthyosaurs suggest that they would not have been able to drag themselves out of water to lay eggs on land, like plesiosaurs. Instead, experts believe that they gave birth to live young in the water. Like baby whales, the ichthyosaurs are believed to have been born tail first so they did not drown during birth. Once the head was out of the mother's body, the young ichthyosaur could swim up to the water surface to take its first breath.

Fossil finds

- Most of what we know about how ichthyosaurs were born comes from the hundreds of amazing fossils with the unborn young of the ichthyosaur inside the body of their parent. At first, scientists, who believed that ichthyosaurs laid eggs, thought that the embryos were examples of ichthyosaur cannibalism, but now we know that they were embryos.

OTHER REPTILES

PTEROSAURS

Flying reptiles called pterosaurs were the first ever vertebrates to take to life in the air. A vertebrate is an animal with a backbone, such as a reptile, mammal, bird, fish or amphibian. At the time when pterosaurs began to fly, there were no birds, only insects.

PTEROSAUR FLIGHT
Pterosaurs first lived in the Triassic, millions of years before the first birds. Instead of front limbs they had wings which were made of skin and supported the very long fourth finger on each hand. The wings were also attached to the sides of the body. These reptiles did not just glide but flew by flapping their wings.

RHAMPHORHYNCHUS
Rhamphorhynchus *lived during the Late Jurassic in Europe and measured about 1 metre (3 feet) from wing-tip to wing-tip. It had long narrow jaws, equipped with many sharp teeth and may have fed on fish. Fossils found in Germany show that the wings were strengthened by thin fibres running through them.*

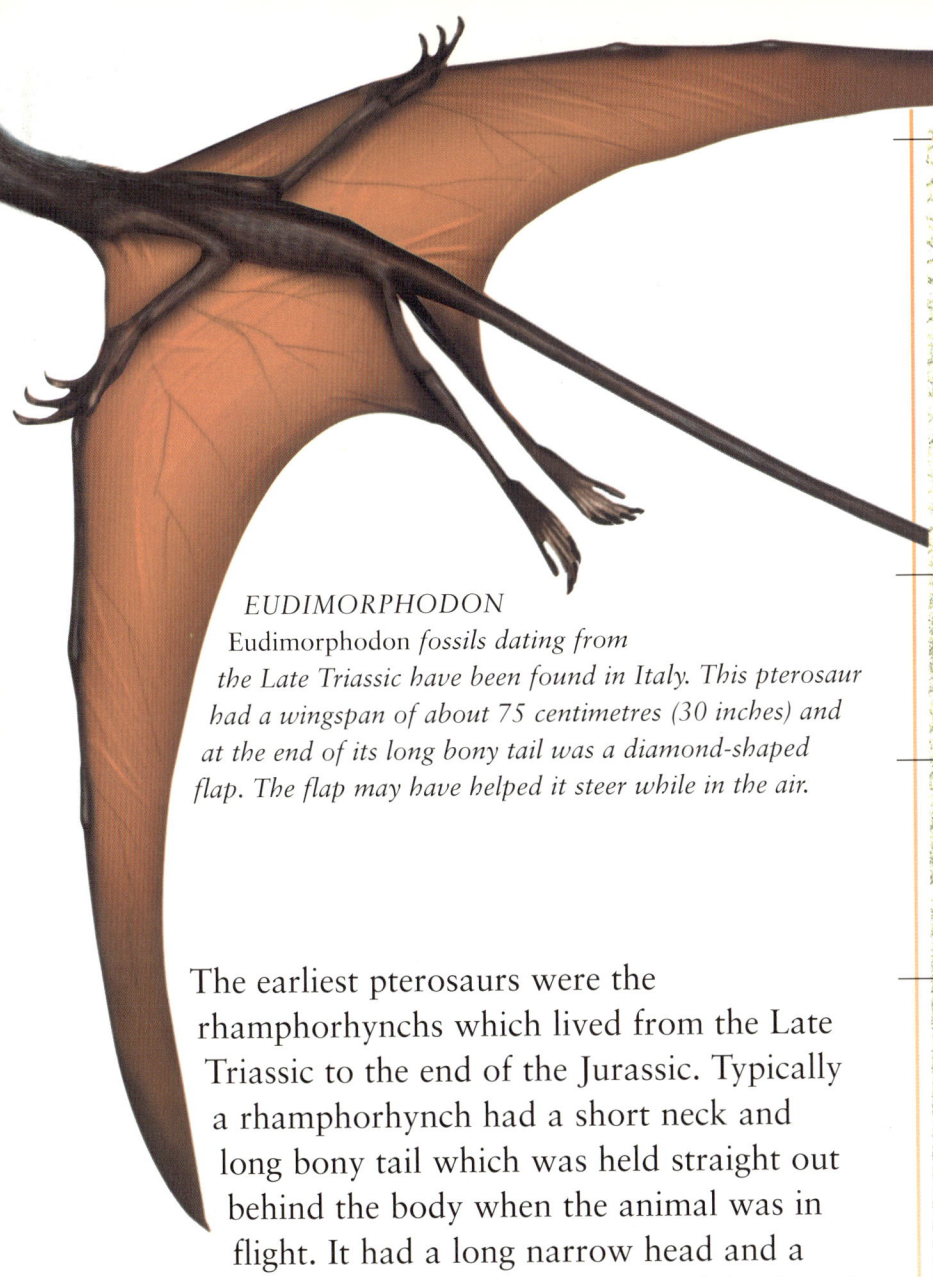

EUDIMORPHODON
Eudimorphodon fossils dating from the Late Triassic have been found in Italy. This pterosaur had a wingspan of about 75 centimetres (30 inches) and at the end of its long bony tail was a diamond-shaped flap. The flap may have helped it steer while in the air.

The earliest pterosaurs were the rhamphorhynchs which lived from the Late Triassic to the end of the Jurassic. Typically a rhamphorhynch had a short neck and long bony tail which was held straight out behind the body when the animal was in flight. It had a long narrow head and a large number of teeth. It probably ate fish, though some may have fed on insects.

- **Brainy pterosaur**
  - *Scaphognathus* fossils show that it may have had a much larger brain than most reptiles. The areas of the brain connected with sight and movement were particularly well developed. This pterosaur lived in the Late Jurassic in Britain and had a wing-span of up to 1 metre (3 feet).

- **Pterosaur sizes**
  - Most of these early pterosaurs were small, ranging from about the size of a sparrow to a seagull.

- **Blood facts**
  - Experts believe that pterosaurs must have been warm-blooded or they would not have had enough energy to fly.

- **Pterosaur facts**
  - Some fossils suggest that the body and wings may have been covered with hair.
  - Pterosaurs had a range of different crests on their head from long, low crests along the beak to sail-shaped, high crests protruding from the skull.

OTHER REPTILES

PTERODACTYLS

During the Jurassic, about 45 million years after the first pterosaurs appeared, a more advanced group, called pterodactyls, evolved. They looked similar to the earlier rhamphorhynchs but had shorter tails and longer necks.

FLYING GIANT
A huge pterosaur, *Quetzalcoatlus* may have been the largest flying vertebrate ever known. Few fossils have been found but they show that *Quetzalcoatlus* may have measured as much as 12 metres (39 feet) from wing-tip to wing-tip. It could probably glide on air currents like large sea birds today.

PTEROSAUR ANATOMY
The later pterosaurs grew much larger than their earlier relatives. One, *Quetzalcoatlus*, was the largest creature ever known to have flown. Such pterosaurs may have been expert soarers, like large sea birds today, travelling long distances over the oceans in search of food. They may not have been able to take off from the ground and might have climbed up to a high spot such as a tree or rock to launch themselves off.

Experts have long argued about how pterosaurs moved on the ground. Some believe that they walked upright on their two back legs, like birds today. Others think that they crawled around on all fours, using the claws on their wings and feet. They would also have used their wing-claws when climbing.

PTERODACTYLUS

This pterodactyl lived in Europe and Africa in the Late Jurassic and had a wing-span of up to 75 centimetres (30 inches). Its long jaws and small sharp teeth would have been ideal for catching fish.

- **The first bird**
  - *Archaeopteryx* was not a pterosaur – it was the first known bird. Fossils show that it had feathered wings like modern birds but that it also had toothed jaws and a bony tail like a reptile. It was probably not a strong flier and may not have been able to take off from the ground. It could have climbed up trees with the help of its wing-claws as well as its feet and jumped off into the air to search for insects to eat. *Archaeopteryx* was about the size of a modern pigeon and lived in Europe. At first, a single feather was discovered in 1860. Since then six more have been found, including an almost complete skeleton.
- **Other pterodactyls**
  - *Pterodaustro* had many bristle-like structures in its jaw that might have been used to strain insects and other small creatures from the water.
  - *Tapejara* had long toothless jaws like pincers that it could have used to pick fruit from the trees.

OTHER REPTILES

MAMMAL-LIKE REPTILES

Mammal-like reptiles are called this because they looked so similar to mammals such as dogs and bears. They first appeared in the Late Carboniferous, long before the dinosaurs. But by the end of the Jurassic the dinosaurs had taken over and all the mammal-like reptiles were extinct.

EARLY MAMMALS
The earliest group of mammal-like reptiles were the pelycosaurs, which first lived during the Late Carboniferous, about 300 million years ago. The first pelycosaurs were small lizard-like creatures but they developed into much larger, more powerful animals such as *Dimetrodon*, a hunter with a sail-like fin on its back. Later came more advanced creatures such as the dicynodonts and cynodonts.

PLANT EATER
Like others of its group, Dicynodon *had two tusk-like teeth in its upper jaw, which it may have used to dig up plants to eat.* Dicynodon *lived in Africa during the Late Permian period and was 1.2 metres (4 feet) long.*

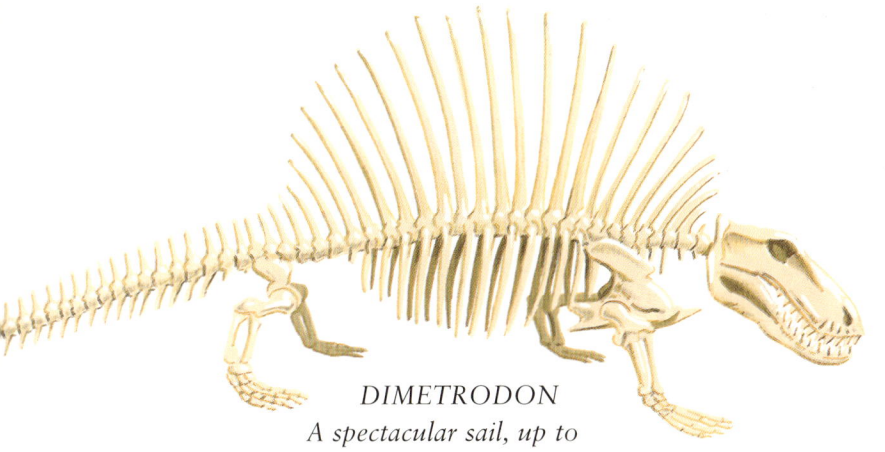

DIMETRODON
A spectacular sail, up to 1 metre (3 feet) high in the centre, rose from the back of this mammal-like reptile. In life the sail was probably covered with skin and may have helped the reptile control its body temperature. Dimetrodon grew to about 3 metres (10 feet) long and lived in western North America.

Dicynodonts were most common in the Late Permian period, before the dinosaurs. They had stocky pig-like bodies and a small tail. Dicynodonts were plant eaters with powerful jaws. The more highly developed structure of the skull allowed them to have stronger jaw muscles than earlier reptiles so they could bite and chew more effectively.

- **Mammal ancestors**
  - Cynodonts were the most successful of all the mammal-like reptiles and survived the longest – until the middle of the Jurassic period. Most important of all, they were the ancestors of mammals – including humans. Like their relatives, dicynodonts, cynodonts had strong jaws but they also had specialized teeth like mammals, for cutting and chewing. Cynodonts may even have had a covering of hair which would have helped to keep them warm.

- **Wolf-like hunter**
  - *Lycaenops* was a fast-running, wolf-like hunter. Like wolves today, it may have hunted in packs, working together to bring down much larger plant eaters. It had strong jaws and big canine teeth. *Lycaenops* lived in South Africa in the Late Permian and was about 1 metre (3 feet) long.

INTRODUCTION TO

The End of the Dinosaurs

Dinosaurs, together with a number of other animals such as pterosaurs, ichthyosaurs, plesiosaurs and ammonites, disappeared for ever at the end of the Cretaceous period, 65 million years ago. Meanwhile, other creatures, including mammals, birds, and many other types of reptiles such as crocodiles, lizards and turtles, survived whatever catastrophe there was.

At the moment no one knows which theory for how the dinosaurs became extinct is correct. It could even be that the truth is a combination of the two. Perhaps dinosaurs and some other creatures were gradually dying out anyway due to climate change and their end was simply hastened by a catastrophe – such as meteorite explosion. What remains a mystery is why some groups of creatures were so badly affected that they disappeared for ever and why others survived.

Theories
- Scientists have come up with many different theories. Some believe that the extinction did not come suddenly and that dinosaurs died out gradually over several million years.
- Other experts believe that the extinctions happened as the result of a giant meteorite crashing to Earth from space. This meteorite may have been 10 kilometres (6 miles) across and a crater has been found near the coast of Mexico that could have been made by such a meteorite. The impact would have caused vast amounts of dust and debris to be thrown into the atmosphere and could have caused major climate change. Huge hurricanes and firestorms would have raged all over the world. Plants would have died and with them plant-eating dinosaurs and their hunters. Rocks from many parts of the world dating from that time contain a layer of a mineral called iridium – which comes from meteorites.

Index

Africa 24, 31, 34
   iguanodonts 36
   pterodactyls 57
   reptiles 58
   stegosaurs 40, 41
Allosaurus 15, 20
ammonites 51, 60
amphibians 7, 9, 54
anchisaurids 29
Andrews, R.C. 13
ankylosaurs 10, 15, 43
Antarctica 10, 35
Archaeopteryx 57
Archelon 49
Argentina 8, 13, 29
Argentinasaurus 7
armoured dinosaurs 42—3
Asia 17, 24, 26, 32, 33
   armoured dinosaurs 43
   duck-billed dinosaurs 38
   horned dinosaurs 45
   iguanodonts 36
   parrot dinosaurs 44
   stegosaurs 40
Australia 35, 36, 51

B
baby dinosaurs 16—17
backbones 54
Barosaurus 10
Baryonyx 15
birds 22, 24—5, 54, 56—7, 60
birth 53
boneheaded dinosaurs 32—3
brachiosaurs 30, 31
Britain 55
Buckland, W. 12

C
camarasaurs 30
cannibalism 19
Carboniferous Period 58
Carcharodontosaurus 21
Carnosaurus 18—19
carrion 19, 26, 27
Centrosaurus 47
ceratopsians 46, 47
ceratosaurs 18, 19
China 12, 21, 23, 33
   fabrosaurs 34
   hypsilophodonts 35
   stegosaurs 41

climate change 61
Coelophysis 19
Compsognathus 18, 19
Cope, E.D. 12, 13
crests 39, 55
Cretaceous Period 9, 16, 18, 23—7, 32—6
   Early 31, 43—4, 51, 53
   Late 38, 42, 44—9, 51, 60
   maniraptorans 22
   Middle 52
   tetanurans 20
   tyrannosaurs 26
crocodiles 7, 48, 49, 60
cryptoclidids 51
cynodonts 58, 59

D
Deinonychus 13, 22
Deinosuchus 48, 49
Dicynodon 58
dicynodonts 58, 59
Dimetrodon 58, 59
dinosaurs
   armoured 42—3
   boneheaded 32—3

duck-billed 38—9
end 60—1
families 16—17, 32—3
horned 44—5, 46—7
hunters 12—13
introduction 6—7
knowledge 10—11
life styles 14—15
meat-eating 18—19
naming 13
parrot-type 44—5
world 8—9
diplodocids 30
Diplodocus 7, 11
dolphins 52
Dromaeosaurus 23
duck-billed dinosaurs 38—9

E
Earth 6
eggs 6, 7, 13, 16—17, 19
   hypsilophodonts 35
   ichthyosaurs 53
   Oviraptor 25, 45
   plesiosaurs 51
elasmosaurs 51
Elasmosaurus 51

embryos 53
end of dinosaurs 60—1
England 15, 34
Eoraptor 8
Eudimorphodon 55
Euoplocephalus 42
Europe 28, 31, 32, 34
   armoured dinosaurs 43
   duck-billed dinosaurs 38
   hypsilophodonts 35
   iguanodonts 36
   pterodactyls 57
   pterosaurs 54
   reptiles 49
   stegosaurs 40
extinction 46, 58, 60—1

F
fabrosaurs 34—5
families 16—17, 32—3
feathers 57
fenestrae 49
fish 9, 15, 19, 51—2
   pterosaurs 54—5
flying dinosaurs 6
flying reptiles 54—5
fossilization 11
fossils 10—11, 13, 18, 23, 35
   ichthyosaurs 53
   Oviraptor 25
   plesiosaurs 51
   pterosaurs 54, 55
   Quetzalcoatlus 56

G
Gallimimus 24
Gasosaurus 21
gastroliths 45
Germany 28, 54
Gigantosaurus 21
giraffes 51
goats 33
Gobi Desert 13, 17
Gondwana 8

H
hadrosaurines 39
hadrosaurs 15
Herrerasaurus 8
Homalocephale 33
homalocephalids 33
horned dinosaurs 44—5, 46—7
humans 59
hunters 12—13
Hypsilophodon 10, 34
hypsilophodonts 34—5

I
ichthyosaurs 6, 9, 51, 52—3, 60
Ichthyosaurus 53
iguanas 13
Iguanodon 10, 13, 37
iguanodonts 36—7
incubation 17
insects 8, 9, 25, 54, 55, 57
irridium 61
Isle of Wight 34
Italy 55

J
jaws 57, 59
Jobara 31
Jurassic Period 8—9, 18, 20—2, 30, 36, 40—1
   brachiosaurs 31
   Early 28, 29, 34, 49, 53
   Late 43, 51, 54—5, 57—8
   Middle 35, 40, 59
   pterodactyls 56
   tetanurans 20

K
kangaroos 35
Kentrosaurus 41
Kronosaurus 51

L
lambeosaurines 39
Lambeosaurus 39
Laurasia 8
Lesothosaurus 34
life styles 14—15
Liopleurodon 7
lizards 6—9, 12, 16, 25, 60
Lycaenops 59

M
Madagascar 8, 13
Maiasaura 16, 17
mammal-like reptiles 58—9
mammals 8—9, 25, 54, 59—60
maniraptorans 22—3

Mantell, G. 12—13, 36
Mantell, M. 12
marine reptiles 7, 9, 50—2
Marsh, O.C. 12, 13
mating 41
meat eaters 7, 8, 14—15, 18—27
Megalosaurus 12
Megazostrodon 9
melanosaurids 29
meteorites 61
Metriorhynchus 49
Mexico 61
Minmi 10
Mongolia 23, 25, 45

N
naming dinosaurs 13
nests 16, 17
nodosaurs 43
North Africa 21
North America 16, 20
   armoured dinosaurs 42, 43
   boneheaded dinosaurs 32, 33
   brachiosaurs 31
   duck-billed dinosaurs 38, 39
   horned dinosaurs 46, 47
   hypsilophodonts 34—5
   iguanodonts 36
   maniraptorans 22, 23
   ornithomimids 24, 25
   reptiles 48, 49, 59

sauropods 30
stegosaurs 40
tyrannosaurs 26, 27
nothosaurs 51

O
ornithischians 6, 7, 35, 40, 43
ornithomimids 24—5
ostrich dinosaurs 24, 25
Ouranosaurus 37
Oviraptor 13, 25, 45
Owen, R. 12, 13

P
pachycephalosaurs 33
palaeontologists 10, 11, 12, 41
Pangaea 8
Parasaurolophus 38
parents 16, 17, 45, 53
parrot dinosaurs 44—5
pelycosaurs 58
penguins 50
Permian Period 58, 59
placodonts 51
plant eaters 7, 9, 14, 28—9
  armoured dinosaurs 43
  duck-billed dinosaurs 39
  fabrosaurs 34—5
  families 16
  iguanodonts 36—7
  maniraptorans 22
  parrot dinosaurs 45
  reptiles 48, 58
  sauropods 30—1

stegosaurs 40—1
tyrannosaurs 26
plateosaurids 29
Plateosaurus 28
plesiosaurids 51
plesiosaurs 50—1, 53, 60
pliosaurs 7, 50—1
Plot, R. 12
predators 15, 18, 21, 35, 43, 47
prosauropods 28, 29
Protoceratops 13, 17, 23, 45
protoceratopsians 45
Psittacosaurus 44
pterodactyls 56—7
Pterodactylus 57
Pterodaustro 57
pterosaurs 6, 9, 54—5, 56, 60

Q
Quetzalcoatlus 56

R
reptiles 6—7, 9, 12—13, 16, 19
  flying 54—5
  mammal-like 58—9
  marine 50—1
  types 37, 48—9, 51, 60
rhamphorhynchs 55, 56
Rhamphorhynchus 54
rhinoceros 47
Riojasaurus 13, 29

S
Sahara Desert 31

saurischians 7, 19, 22, 24, 27
  plant eaters 28
  sauropods 30
sauropods 7, 14, 15, 20, 28, 30—1
Saurornithoides 22
Scaphognathus 55
sea turtles 49, 50
seals 51
sheep 33
Shonisaurus 52
skeletons 6, 7, 11, 13, 19
skin 6, 25, 41, 49
South Africa 59
South America 21, 29, 38
Staurikosaurus 10
Stegoceras 33
stegosaurs 40—1
Stegosaurus 40, 41
Struthiomimus 25
Styracosaurus 47
swimming dinosaurs 6

T
Tapejara 57
Tarbosaurus 26
teeth 14, 15, 27, 29
Teleosaurus 49
Terrestrisuchus 49
tetanurans 20—1
theropods 18, 19
tortoises 48
Triassic Period 8, 9, 18—19
  Early 52
  Late 28—9, 48, 52, 55
  meat eaters 19

placodonts 51
pterosaurs 54
reptiles 49
Triceratops 46, 47
Tröodon 22, 23
tröodontids 22, 23
Tuojiangosaurus 10, 41
turtles 9, 16, 48, 49, 50, 51, 60
tyrannosaurs 15, 23, 26—7, 47
Tyrannosaurus 7, 10, 13
  family 27
  structure 26
tetanurans 21

U
United States 13, 35

V
Velociraptor 15, 23
vertebrates 54

W
whales 53
wolves 59

Y
Yangchuanosaurus 21